'Better mad
with the crowd
than sane
all alone . . .'

BALTASAR GRACIÁN
Born 1601, Aragon, Spain
Died 1658, Aragon, Spain

Selection taken from *The Pocket Oracle and Art of Prudence*,
first published in 1647.

GRACIÁN IN PENGUIN CLASSICS
The Pocket Oracle and Art of Prudence

BALTASAR GRACIÁN

How to Use Your Enemies

Translated by
Jeremy Robbins

PENGUIN BOOKS

PENGUIN CLASSICS

Published by the Penguin Group
Penguin Books Ltd, 80 Strand, London WC2R ORL, England
Penguin Group (USA) Inc., 375 Hudson Street, New York, New York 10014, USA
Penguin Group (Canada), 90 Eglinton Avenue East, Suite 700, Toronto, Ontario,
Canada M4P 2Y3 (a division of Pearson Penguin Canada Inc.)
Penguin Ireland, 25 St Stephen's Green, Dublin 2, Ireland
(a division of Penguin Books Ltd)
Penguin Group (Australia), 707 Collins Street, Melbourne, Victoria 3008, Australia
(a division of Pearson Australia Group Pty Ltd)
Penguin Books India Pvt Ltd, 11 Community Centre, Panchsheel Park,
New Delhi – 110 017, India
Penguin Group (NZ), 67 Apollo Drive, Rosedale, North Shore 0632, New Zealand
(a division of Pearson New Zealand Ltd)
Penguin Books (South Africa) (Pty) Ltd, Block D, Rosebank Office Park,
181 Jan Smuts Avenue, Parktown North, Gauteng 2193, South Africa

Penguin Books Ltd, Registered Offices: 80 Strand, London WC2R ORL, England

www.penguin.com

This selection published in Penguin Classics 2015
002

Translation copyright © Jeremy Robbins, 2011

The moral right of the translator has been asserted

Set in 9.5/13 pt Baskerville 10 Pro
Typeset by Jouve (UK), Milton Keynes
Printed in Great Britain by Clays Ltd, St Ives plc

A CIP catalogue record for this book is available from the British Library

ISBN: 978–0–141–39827–3

www.greenpenguin.co.uk

In your affairs, create suspense. Admiration at their novelty means respect for your success. It's neither useful nor pleasurable to show all your cards. Not immediately revealing everything fuels anticipation, especially when a person's elevated position means expectations are greater. It bespeaks mystery in everything and, with this very secrecy, arouses awe. Even when explaining yourself, you should avoid complete frankness, just as you shouldn't open yourself up to everyone in all your dealings. Cautious silence is the refuge of good sense. A decision openly declared is never respected; instead, it opens the way to criticism, and if things turn out badly, you'll be unhappy twice over. Imitate divinity's way of doing things to keep people attentive and alert.

*

Knowledge and courage contribute in turn to greatness. Since they are immortal, they immortalize. You are as much as you know, and a wise person can do anything. A person without knowledge is a world in darkness. Judgement and strength, eyes and hands; without courage, wisdom is sterile.

*

Make people depend on you. An image is made sacred not by its creator but by its worshipper. The shrewd would rather people needed them than thanked them. To put your trust in vulgar gratitude is to devalue courteous hope, for whilst hope remembers, gratitude forgets. More can be gained from dependence than from courtesy; once thirst is quenched, people turn their backs on the fountain, and an orange once squeezed is tossed in the mud. When dependence ends, so does harmony, and with it esteem. Let experience's first lesson be to maintain and never satisfy dependence, keeping even royalty always in need of you. But you shouldn't go to the extreme of being so silent as to cause error, or make someone else's problems incurable for your own benefit.

*

The height of perfection. No one is born complete; perfect yourself and your activities day by day until you become a truly consummate being, your talents and your qualities all perfected. This will be evident in the excellence of your taste, the refinement of your intellect, the maturity of your judgement, the purity of your will. Some never manage to be complete; something is always missing. Others take a long time. The consummate man, wise in word and sensible in deed, is admitted into, and even sought out for, the singular company of the discreet.

*

Avoid outdoing your superior. All triumphs are despised, and triumphing over your superior is either stupid or fatal. Superiority has always been detested, especially by our superiors. Caution can usually hide ordinary advantages, just as it conceals beauty with a touch of carelessness. There will always be someone ready to admit others have better luck or temperaments, but no one, and especially not a sovereign, that someone has greater ingenuity. For this is the sovereign attribute and any crime against it is lese-majesty. Sovereigns, then, desire sovereignty over what matters most. Princes like to be helped, but not surpassed. Advice should be offered as if a reminder of what they've forgotten, not an insight that they've never had. The stars teach us such subtlety, for though they are children of the sun and shine brilliantly, they never compete with it in all its radiance.

*

Belie your national defects. Water acquires the good and bad qualities of the channels it passes through, people those of the country where they're born. Some owe more than others to their birthplace, for the heavens were more propitious to them there. No country, even the most civilized, is free from some national failing which neighbouring countries will always criticize, either for advantage or solace. It's a skilful triumph to correct, or at least to conceal, these national faults; you'll gain credit as unique among your countrymen, for what's least expected has always been more esteemed. There are also defects of lineage, status, occupation and age which, if they all appear in one person and are not carefully forestalled, will produce an unbearable monster.

*

Deal with people from whom you can learn. Let friendly interchange be a school of erudition, and conversation, civilized instruction. Make friends your teachers, joining learning's usefulness and conversation's pleasure. The intelligent combine two pleasures, enjoying the applause that greets what they say and the instruction received from what they hear. Usually, we are drawn to someone through our own interest, but here, that interest is ennobled. The circumspect frequent the company of eminent individuals whose houses are theatres of greatness rather than palaces of vanity. There are those renowned for their discretion whose example and behaviour are oracles in all matters of greatness and whose entourages are also courtly academies of good and gallant discretion.

*

Nature and art, material and craft. Beauty always needs a helping hand, and perfection is rough without the polish of artifice. It helps what is bad and perfects what is good. Nature usually lets us down when we need it most; let us then turn to art. Without it, our nature even at its best lacks refinement, and when culture is lacking, perfection remains incomplete. Everyone seems coarse without artifice, and everyone needs its polish in all areas to be perfect.

*

Reality and manner. Substance is insufficient, circumstance is also vital. A bad manner ruins everything, even justice and reason. A good manner makes up for everything: it gilds a 'no', sweetens truth, and beautifies old age itself. How something is done plays a key role in all affairs, and a good manner is a winning trick. Graceful conduct is the chief ornament of life; it gets you out of any tight situation.

*

Have intelligent support. The good fortune of the powerful: to be accompanied by outstanding minds that can save them from tight spots caused by their own ignorance and fight difficult battles for them. It shows exceptional greatness to make use of wise people, far better than the barbarous preference of Tigranes who wanted conquered kings as his servants. A new type of mastery over what's best in life: skilfully make those whom nature made superior your servants. There's much to know and life is short, and a life without knowledge is not a life. It's a singular skill effortlessly to learn much from many, gaining knowledge from all. Then you can speak in a meeting for many or, through your words, as many wise people as advised you will speak. You'll gain a reputation as an oracle through the sweat of others. Your learned helpers first select the subject, and then distil their knowledge and present it to you. If you can't have wisdom as your servant, at least be on intimate terms.

*

Vary your procedure. Not always the same way, so as to confound those observing you, especially if they are rivals. Don't always fulfil your declared intentions, for others will seize on your predictability, anticipating and frustrating your actions. It's easy to kill a bird that flies straight, but not one that twists and turns. But don't always do the opposite of what you say, for the trick will be understood the second time around. Malice is always lying in wait – great subtlety is needed to mislead it. Sharp players never move the piece their opponents are expecting, and especially not the one they want them to.

*

A person born in the right century. Truly outstanding people depend on their times. Not all were born at the time they deserved, and many, though they were, didn't manage to take advantage of it. Some were worthy of a better century, for every good doesn't triumph at all times. Everything has its time; even what's outstanding is subject to changing taste. But wisdom has the advantage of being eternal, and if this is not its century, many others will be.

*

Find everyone's weak spot. This is the art of moving people's wills. It consists more in skill than determination – a knowledge of how to get inside each person. Everyone's will has its own particular predilection, all different according to the variety of tastes. We all idolize something: for some, esteem; for others, self-interest; and for most, pleasure. The trick to influencing people lies in knowing what they idolize. Knowing each person's driving impulse is like having the key to their will. You should go direct to what most motivates a person, normally something base rather than anything noble, for there are more self-indulgent people than self-controlled ones in the world. You should first divine someone's character, then touch upon their fixation, and take control of their driving passion which, without fail, will defeat their free will.

*

Know the fortunate, to befriend them, and the unfortunate, to shun them. Misfortune is normally the crime of fools – and nothing is more contagious. You should never open the door to the smallest ill, for others, both many and greater, will come in after it and ambush you. The greatest trick is to know which cards to throw away: the lowest card that wins the current game is worth more than the highest that won an earlier one. If in doubt, a good move is to attach yourself to the wise and the prudent, for sooner or later they'll meet with good fortune.

*

Know how to leave things to one side, for if knowing how to refuse is one of life's great lessons, an even greater one is knowing how to say no to yourself, to important people, and in business. There are non-essential activities, moths of precious time, and it's worse to take an interest in irrelevant things than do nothing at all. To be circumspect, it's not enough to interfere; it's more important to make sure others don't interfere in your affairs. Don't so belong to others that you don't belong to yourself. Even friends should not be abused; you shouldn't want more from them than they're willing to concede. Any extreme is a vice, and especially in dealings with others. Sensible moderation is the best way to maintain goodwill and respect because ever-precious dignity won't be worn away. Be free in spirit, passionate about all that's fine, and never sin against your own good taste.

*

Know your key quality, your outstanding gift. Cultivate it, and improve the rest. Everyone could have been pre-eminent in something, if they had been aware of their best quality. Identify your key attribute and redouble its use. In some this is their judgement, in others courage. Most people misuse their capabilities, and so achieve superiority in nothing. What passion rushes to flatter, time is slow to disillusion us about.

*

Quit whilst fortune is smiling, as all good gamblers do. A graceful retreat is as important as a brave assault, safeguarding achievements once these are enough, and especially when they're more than enough. Always be suspicious of unbroken good fortune; far safer is fortune that's mixed, and for it to be bittersweet even whilst you are enjoying it. The more blessings there are rushing towards us, the greater the risk of them stumbling and bringing everything down. The intensity of fortune's favour sometimes compensates for the brevity of its duration. It quickly grows tired of carrying someone on its shoulders.

*

Be in people's good graces. It's a great thing to earn people's admiration, but more so their affection. This is partly a matter of luck, but mostly of effort; it begins with the first and is pursued with the second. Outstanding talent is not enough, although people imagine that it's easy to win affection once respect has been won. For benevolence,

9

beneficence is required. Do endless good; good words, better deeds; love, in order to be loved. Courtesy is the greatest, most politic spell the great can cast. Reach for great deeds first, then for the pen; go from the sword to sheets of paper, for the favour of writers, which exists, is eternal.

*

Think with the few and speak with the many. To want to go against the current is as impossible for the wise as it is easy for the reckless. Only a Socrates could undertake this. Dissent is taken as an insult since it condemns another's judgement. Those offended multiply, either because of the point criticized or the person who'd endorsed it. Truth is for the few; deception is as common as it is vulgar. The wise cannot be identified by what they say in public, since they never speak there with their own voice but following common stupidity, however much their inner thoughts contradict this. The sensible flee being contradicted as much as contradicting: what they're quick to censure, they're slow to publicize. Thought is free; it cannot and should not be coerced. It retreats into the sanctuary of silence, and if it sometimes breaks this, it only does so among the select and the wise.

*

Caution – use it, but don't abuse it. Don't affect it, far less reveal it: all art should be concealed, for it's suspect, and especially the art of caution, which is odious. Deceit is widely used; suspicion should be everywhere but without revealing itself, for this would occasion distrust: it causes affront, provokes revenge, and arouses unimagined troubles. Reflective behaviour is of great advantage to our deeds: there is no greater proof of reason. An action's absolute perfection is secured by the mastery with which it is executed.

*

Never lose your composure. A prime aim of good sense: never lose your cool. This is proof of true character, of a perfect heart, because magnanimity is difficult to perturb. Passions are the humours of the mind and any imbalance in them unsettles good sense, and if this illness leads us to open our mouths, it will endanger our reputation. Be so in control of yourself that, whether things are going well or badly, nobody can accuse you of being perturbed and all can admire your superiority.

*

Know how to adapt yourself. You don't need to appear equally intelligent to all, nor should you employ more effort than is necessary. With knowledge and excellence, nothing should be squandered. A good falconer releases only as many birds as are needed for the chase. Don't continually flaunt your qualities or there'll be nothing left to admire. There must always be something novel with which to dazzle, for people who reveal something new each day keep interest alive and never allow the limits of their great abilities to be discovered.

*

Leave a good impression. In the house of Fortune, if you enter through pleasure's door, you'll leave through sorrow's, and vice versa. Pay attention to how things end, then, taking greater care to make a good exit than a widely applauded entrance. It's common for lucky people to have very favourable beginnings and truly tragic ends. The aim is not to have your entrance applauded by the rabble, for everyone's is greeted this way. What matters rather is the general feeling your exit arouses, for few are missed once gone. Good fortune rarely accompanies those on their way out; she is as polite to those who are arriving as she is rude to those who are leaving.

*

Make sure of a successful outcome. Some focus more on going about things the right way than on achieving their goal. But the discredit that comes with failure outweighs any credit gained by such diligence. Whoever wins need offer no explanations. Most people don't see the precise circumstances, only a good or bad outcome. Reputation is therefore never lost when goals are achieved. A successful conclusion makes everything golden, however mistaken the means. For it shows wisdom to go against received wisdom when there's no other way to achieve a happy outcome.

*

Know how to refuse. Not everything has to be granted, nor to everyone. This is as important as knowing how to grant something, and is a vital necessity for rulers. Your manner is important here: one person's 'no' is valued more than another's 'yes', because a gilded 'no' satisfies far more than a blunt 'yes'. Many are always ready to say 'no', turning everything sour. 'No' is always their first reaction, and although they subsequently grant everything, they are not held in esteem because of the taste left by the initial refusal. Things shouldn't be refused in one fell swoop; let disappointment sink in gradually. Nor should refusals be categoric, for dependants then give up all hope. Always let there be a few crumbs of hope to temper the bitterness of refusal. Let courtesy make up for the lack of favour, and fine words the lack of deeds. 'Yes' and 'no' are quick to say, and require much thought.

*

Know how to be evasive. This is the escape route of sensible people. With the charm of a witty phrase, they can normally extricate themselves from the most intricate labyrinth. They can avoid the most difficult confrontation with a smile: the courage of the greatest of the great captains was based on this. A polite tactic in refusing is to change the subject, and there's no greater act of caution than to conceal that you have understood.

*

Know how to be all things to all people. A discreet Proteus: with the learned, learned, and with the devout, devout. A great art to win everyone over, since similarity creates goodwill. Observe each person's temperament and tune yours to it. Whether with a serious or a jovial person, go with the current, undergoing a transformation that is politic – and essential for those in positions of dependency. Such vital subtlety requires great ability. It is less difficult for the universal man with his wide-ranging intellect and taste.

*

Take care when gathering information. We live mainly on information. We see very little for ourselves and live on others' testimony. Hearing is truth's last entry point, and a lie's first. Truth is normally seen and rarely heard. It rarely reaches us unadulterated, especially when it comes from far off. It is always tinged with the emotions through which it has passed. Passion tints everything it touches, making it odious or pleasing. It always tries to make an impression, so consider carefully a person offering praise, and even more so someone uttering abuse. The greatest attention is needed here to discover their intention by knowing beforehand where they're coming from. Let caution weigh up what's missing and what's false.

*

Dazzle anew. This is the privilege of the phoenix. Excellence normally grows old, and with it fame. Custom diminishes admiration, and mediocre novelty usually trumps aged pre-eminence. Valour, ingenuity, fortune, indeed everything, should be reborn. Dare to dazzle anew, rising repeatedly like the sun, shining in different fields, so that your absence in one area awakens desire and your novel appearance in another, applause.

*

Know how to use your enemies. You must know how to take hold of everything – not by the blade, which wounds, but by the hilt, which defends. This applies especially to envy. Enemies are of more use to the wise man than friends are to the fool. Ill will usually levels mountains of difficulty which goodwill would balk at tackling. The greatness of many has been fashioned thanks to malicious enemies. Flattery is more harmful than hatred, for the latter is an effective remedy for the flaws that the former conceals. Sensible people fashion a mirror from spite, more truthful than that of affection, and reduce or correct their defects, for great caution is needed when living on the frontier of envy and ill will.

*

Forestall malicious gossip. The mob is many-headed, with many malicious eyes and many slanderous tongues. Sometimes a rumour tarnishing the best reputation spreads through it, and if this results in your becoming a byword, it will destroy your name. The basis for this is normally some obvious defect, some ridiculous shortcomings, which are popular material for gossip. There are flaws secretly exposed by private envy to public malice, for there are malevolent tongues that destroy a great reputation more quickly with a joke than with open effrontery. It's very easy to gain a bad reputation, for badness is easy to believe and hard to erase. The sensible man should avoid such things and carefully forestall the insolence of the mob, for prevention is easier than cure.

*

Let your manner be lofty, endeavour to make it sublime. A great man's conduct should not be petty. You should never go into minute details, especially with unpleasant things, because although it's an advantage to notice everything casually, it isn't to want to inquire into every last thing. You should normally act with a noble generality, which is a form of gallantry. A large part of ruling is dissimulation; you should pass over most things that occur among your family, your friends and particularly your enemies. Triviality is annoying, and in a person's character, tedious. To keep coming back to a disagreement is a kind of mania. Normally, each person's behaviour follows their heart and their talents.

*

Understand yourself: your temperament, intellect, opinions, emotions. You can't be master of yourself if you don't first understand yourself. There are mirrors for the face, but none for the spirit: let discreet self-reflection be yours. And when you cease to care about your external image, focus on the inner one to correct and improve it. Know how strong your good sense and perspicacity are for any undertaking and evaluate your capacity for overcoming obstacles. Fathom your depths and weigh up your capacity for all things.

*

Unfathomable abilities. The circumspect man, if he wants to be venerated by everyone, should prevent the true depths of his knowledge or his courage being plumbed. He should allow himself to be known, but not fully understood. No one should establish the limits of his abilities, because of the danger of having their illusions shattered. He should never allow anyone to grasp everything about him. Greater veneration is created by conjecture and uncertainty over the extent of our ability than by firm evidence of this, however vast it might be.

*

On moral sense. It is the throne of reason, the foundation of prudence, and with it, success is easy. It's heaven's gift – the most wished for, because the greatest and the best. The most important piece of armour, so vital it's the only one whose absence is called a loss. Its lack is always noted first. All life's actions depend on its influence, and all seek its approval, for everything must be carried out with common sense. It consists of an innate propensity for all that most conforms to reason, and is always wedded to what's most right.

*

Conceal your wishes. Passions are breaches in the mind. The most practical kind of knowledge is dissimulation; whoever plays their hand openly runs the risk of losing. Let the reserve of the cautious compete against the scrutiny of the perceptive; against the sharp eyes of the lynx, the ink of the cuttlefish. Don't let your desires be known so that they won't be anticipated, either by opposition or flattery.

*

Half the world is laughing at the other half, and all are fools. Either everything is good or everything bad, depending on people's opinions. What one pursues, another flees.

Whoever wants to make their own opinion the measure of all things is an insufferable fool. Perfection doesn't depend on one person's approval: tastes are as plentiful as faces, and as varied. There's not a single failing without its advocate. Nor should we lose heart if something doesn't please someone, for there'll always be someone else it does. But their applause shouldn't go to our heads, for others will condemn such praise. The measure of true satisfaction is the approval of reputable men who are experts in the relevant field. Life doesn't depend on any one opinion, any one custom, or any one century.

*

Understand what different jobs entail. They are all different and you need great knowledge and observation here. Some require courage, others subtlety. Those that depend on integrity are easier to handle, those on artifice, harder. With the right disposition, nothing else is needed for the former; but all the care and vigilance in the world are not enough for the latter. To govern people is a demanding job, and fools and madmen more so. Twice the wit is needed to deal with someone with none. A job that demands complete dedication, has fixed hours and is repetitive is intolerable; better is one which is free from boredom and which combines variety and importance, because change is refreshing. The best are those where dependency on others is minimal. The worst, one where you are held to account, both in this world and the next.

*

Don't be tedious. People with only one concern and only one subject are usually boring. Brevity flatters and opens more doors: it gains in courtesy what it loses in concision. What's good, if brief, is twice as good. Even bad things, if brief, are not so bad. Paring things down to their essence achieves more than verbosity. It's a commonplace that a tall person is rarely wise – not so much long-legged, as long-winded. There are those who, rather than embellish the world, are mere obstacles, worthless ornaments shunned by all. The discreet person should avoid being a hindrance, especially to the most powerful who are always very busy; worse to annoy one of them than the rest of the world. What's well said, is quickly said.

*

A short cut to being a true person: know how to rub shoulders with others. Interaction is very effective: custom and taste can be learnt, character and even ingenuity can rub off on you without your knowing. Let the impulsive get together with those who are restrained, and similarly other opposite temperaments. In this way, a proper balance will be effortlessly achieved. To know how to accommodate is a great skill. The alternation of opposites beautifies and sustains creation, and if it creates harmony in the natural world, even more so in the moral sphere. Make use of this politic advice when choosing friends and helpers, for from such communication between extremes, a discreet balance will be achieved.

*

Don't hang around to be a setting sun. The sensible person's maxim: abandon things before they abandon you. Know how to turn an ending into a triumph. Sometimes the sun itself, whilst still shining brilliantly, goes behind a cloud so nobody can see it setting, leaving people in suspense over whether it has or not. To avoid being slighted, avoid being seen to decline. Don't wait until everyone turns their back on you, burying you alive to regret but dead to esteem. Someone sharp retires a racehorse at the right time, not waiting until everyone laughs when it falls in mid-race. Let beauty astutely shatter her mirror when the time is right, not impatiently and too late when she sees her own illusions shattered in it.

*

Have friends. They are a second self. To a friend, another friend is always good and wise; between friends, everything turns out well. You are worth as much as others say you are, and to win their good words, win their hearts. Performing a service for another works like a charm, and the best way to win friends is to do people favours. The greatest and the best that we have depends on others.

You must live with either friends or enemies. You should make a new friend every day, if not a confidant, then at least a supporter, for if you have chosen well, some will later become confidants.

*

Win affection. Even the first and highest Cause, in its most important affairs, foresees this need and works towards it. Win someone's affection and their respect will follow. Some so trust merit that they underestimate diligence. But caution knows full well that without people's favour, merit alone is the longest route to take. Goodwill facilitates everything and makes good all deficiencies. It doesn't always take certain qualities – like courage, integrity, wisdom and even discretion – for granted, but will grant them. It never sees faults because it doesn't want to. It usually arises from some material connection, whether temperament, race, family, nationality or employment, or from a more sublime, intangible one, such as talent, duty, reputation or merit. The difficulty lies in gaining it, for it's easy to preserve. You can diligently acquire it and learn how to profit from it.

*

In good fortune prepare for bad. It's sensible to make provision for winter in the summer, and far easier. Favours are cheap then, and friends abundant. It's good to store things up against bad times, for adversity is costly and in need of everything. Have friends and grateful people set aside, for some day you will appreciate what you barely notice now. Villainy never has any friends, disowning them in prosperity, and in adversity being disowned.

*

Get used to the bad temperaments of those you deal with, like getting used to ugly faces. This is advisable in situations of dependency. There are horrible people you can neither live with nor live without. It's a necessary skill, therefore, to get used to them, as to ugliness, so you're not surprised each time their harshness manifests itself. At first they'll frighten you, but gradually your initial horror will disappear and caution will anticipate or tolerate the unpleasantness.

*

Live according to common practice. Even knowledge must keep in fashion; when it's not, you need to know how to appear ignorant. Reasoning and taste change with the times. You shouldn't reason and debate in an old-fashioned way and your taste should be up-to-the-minute. The preference of the majority sets the standard in all things. Follow it whilst it lasts, and move towards eminence. A sensible person must adapt the trappings of both body and soul to the fashion of the times, even if the past seems better. Only in matters of goodness does this rule of life not apply, for you should always practise virtue. Telling the truth and keeping your word are unknown today and seem like things from the past. Good men, though always loved, seem relics of better times, and so even if there happen to be any, they're not emulated because they're not in fashion. The misfortune of your century, that virtue is taken as unusual and malice as the norm! Let those with discretion live as they can, if not as they would prefer, and consider what fortune has given them to be better than what it has denied.

*

Be desired. Few win universal favour; if they win the favour of the wise, it's fortunate. Those on the way out are normally held in lukewarm esteem. There are ways to merit the prize of affection: eminence in your occupation and in your skills is a sure way, and an affable manner is effective. Make the eminent job depend on you so that people see that the job needed you, not you the job. Some confer honour on their position; others have honour conferred on them by it. It's no advantage to be thought good because your successor was bad, since this is not unqualified desire for you, but hatred for the other.

*

The fool is not someone who does something foolish, but someone who, once this is done, doesn't know how to hide it. Your emotions need to be concealed, and even more so your faults. Everyone errs, but with this difference: the shrewd dissimulate what they've done, while fools blab about what they're about to do. Reputation is more a matter of caution than of deeds; if you're not pure, be cautious. A great person's mistakes are observed more closely, like the eclipses of the largest planets. The only things that shouldn't be disclosed in a friendship are your faults; were it possible, these shouldn't even be disclosed to yourself. But another rule of life can be helpful here: know how to forget.

*

Reconsider things. Taking a second look at things provides security, especially when the solution isn't obvious. Take your time, whether to grant something or to improve your situation – new reasons to confirm and corroborate your personal judgement will appear. If it's a question of giving, then a gift is more valued because wisely given than quickly given; something long desired is always more appreciated. If you must refuse, then it allows time to think how, and for your refusal to taste less bitter, because more mature and considered. More often than not, once the initial desire for something has cooled, a refusal will not be felt as a rebuff. If someone asks for something quickly, delay granting it, which is a trick to deflect attention elsewhere.

*

Better mad with the crowd than sane all alone, say politicians. For if everyone is mad, you'll be different to none, and if good sense stands alone, it will be taken as madness. To go with the flow is so important. The greatest form of knowledge is, on occasion, not to know, or to affect not to know. You have to live with others, and most are ignorant. To live alone, you must be either very like God or a complete animal. But I would modify the aphorism and say: better sane with the majority than mad all alone. For some want to be unique in their fantastical illusions.

*

Have double of life's necessities. This is to double life. Don't depend on just one person, or limit yourself to a single resource, however excellent. Everything should be doubled, and especially the sources of advantage, favour and pleasure. The mutability of the moon pervades everything and sets a limit on all permanence, especially in areas that depend on our frail human will. Let your reserves help you against the fragility of life, and let a key rule of the art of living be to double the sources of your own benefit and comfort. Just as nature doubled the most important and exposed parts of the body, so human skill should double those things on which we depend.

*

The art of leaving things alone. Especially when the seas of public or personal life are stormiest. There are whirlwinds in the affairs of men, tempests of the will, and it makes good sense to retire and wait things out in a safe harbour.

Remedies often make troubles worse. Let nature or morality take its course. The wise doctor needs to know when to prescribe something and when not, and often the art lies in not applying any remedy at all. Simply sitting back can be a way of calming the whirlwinds of the mob. Yielding to time now will lead to victory later. A spring's water is easily muddied; you will never make it clear by trying to, only by leaving it well alone. There is no better remedy for disorder than to let it run its course; it will then disappear on its own.

*

Know your unlucky days, for they exist. Nothing will work out right and, even though you change your game, your bad luck will remain. After a few moves you should recognize bad luck, and then withdraw, realizing whether it's your lucky day or not. Even understanding has its moments, for no one is knowledgeable on all occasions. It takes good fortune to reason successfully, just as to write a letter well. All perfection depends on the opportune moment. Even beauty is not always in fashion. Discretion contradicts itself, sometimes falling short, sometimes going too far. To work out well, everything depends on the right time. Just as on some days everything turns out badly, on others it all goes well – and with less effort. It's as though everything has already been done; your ingenuity and character are perfectly aligned with your lucky star. Take advantage of such occasions and don't waste a single moment of them. But a judicious man given one obstacle shouldn't declare it a bad day, or a good one given the reverse, for the former might just be a setback, and the latter, luck.

*

Don't support the worse side out of stubbornness, simply because your opponent has already chosen the better one. The battle will be lost before it's begun and you'll inevitably have to surrender, scorned. You'll never come out best by supporting the worst. Your opponent showed astuteness in anticipating the better side, and you'd be stupid in then deciding to support the worse. Those obstinate in deeds are more stubborn than those obstinate in words, for actions carry more risk than words. The stupidity of stubborn people is seen in their not recognizing what's true or advantageous, preferring argument and contradiction. The circumspect are always on the side of reason, not passion, having got in first to support the best or, if not, having subsequently improved their position, for if their opponents are fools, their very stupidity will make them change course, switch sides, and thereby worsen their position. The only way to get your opponent to stop supporting what's best is to support it yourself, for their stupidity will then make them drop it, and their stubbornness will be their downfall.

*

Go in supporting the other person's interests so as to come out achieving your own. This is a strategy for achieving what you want. Even in matters concerning heaven, Christian teachers recommend such holy astuteness. It's an important kind of dissimulation, because the perceived benefit is just the bait to catch another's will. They'll think you are furthering their own aims, but this will be no more than a means of furthering your own. You should never enter into anything recklessly, especially when there's an undercurrent of danger. With people whose first word is usually 'no', it's also best to conceal your true intentions so that they won't focus on the difficulties of saying 'yes', especially when you sense their aversion to doing so. This piece of advice belongs with those about concealed intentions, for all involve extreme subtlety.

*

Don't expose your sore finger, or everything will knock against it. Don't complain about your sore points, for malice always attacks where our weaknesses hurt most. Getting annoyed will only serve to spur on someone else's enjoyment. The ill-intentioned are searching for a pretext to get your back up. Their dart-like insinuations aim to discover where you hurt, and they'll try a thousand different ways until they hit upon your most sensitive point. The circumspect pretend not to notice and never reveal their troubles, whether their own or their family's, for even fortune occasionally likes to hit where it hurts most, and it always cuts to the quick. You should therefore never reveal what causes you pain or pleasure, so that the former may quickly end and the latter long continue.

*

Don't be inaccessible. Nobody is so perfect that they don't sometimes need advice. Someone who refuses to listen is an incurable fool. The most independent person must still accept the need for friendly advice; even a monarch must be willing to be taught. There are individuals beyond all help because they are inaccessible and who come unstuck because nobody dares to stop them. The most self-sufficient person must leave a door open to friendship, from where all help will come. You need a friend of sufficient influence over you to be able to advise and admonish you freely. Your trust and high opinion of their loyalty and prudence should place them in this position of authority. Though such authority and respect shouldn't be handed to all and sundry, have in caution's innermost room a confidant, a faithful mirror, whose correction you value when disillusionment is necessary.

*

Know how to deflect trouble on to someone else. Having a shield against ill will is a great trick of rulers. To have someone else who can be criticized for mistakes and chastised by gossipmongers is a sign of superior skill, not lack of competence as malice thinks. Not everything can turn out well, nor can everyone be pleased. Have a fall guy, therefore, someone who, at the expense of their own ambition, can be a target for your misfortunes.

*

Think ahead: today for tomorrow, and even for many days after that. The greatest foresight is to have abundant time for it. For the far-sighted, nothing is unexpected; there are no tight spots for those who are prepared. Don't save your reason for when difficulties arise, use it well before that. Anticipate critical times with mature reflection. The pillow is a silent Sibyl and sleeping on things is better than lying awake under their weight. Some act first and think later, which is to search for excuses rather than consequences. Others think neither before nor after. The whole of life should be a process of deliberation to choose the right course. Reflection and foresight provide the means of living in anticipation.

*

Never be associated with someone who can cast you in a poor light, whether because they're better or worse than you. The more perfect they are, the higher their esteem. They will always play the lead role, and you a secondary one, and if you win any esteem, it will simply be their leftovers. The moon on its own stands out among the stars, but when the sun comes out, it either doesn't appear or it disappears. Never consort with someone who eclipses you, only with someone who enhances you. In this way Martial's discreet Fabulla was able to appear beautiful and to shine amidst the ugliness and slovenliness of her maids. Similarly, don't take the risk of keeping bad company, and don't honour others at the cost of your own reputation. To improve yourself, associate with the eminent; once perfected, with the mediocre.

*

Avoid stepping into great men's shoes. And if you do, be sure of your own superiority. To equal your predecessor you will need to be worth twice as much. Just as it's a good strategy to make sure your successor is such that people will miss you, so also to make sure your predecessor doesn't eclipse you. It's difficult to fill the void left by someone great because the past always seems better; even being their equal isn't enough, because they'll always have the advantage of having come first. To topple someone's greater reputation, then, you need qualities above and beyond theirs.

*

Choose your friends: they should become so after being examined by discretion, tested by fortune, and certified not simply by your will but your understanding. Although the most important thing in life, it's usually the one over which least care is taken: some are forced upon us, most are the result of pure chance. A person is defined by the

friends they have, and the wise never make friends with
fools. But liking someone's company need not suggest
true intimacy – it can simply mean enjoying their humour
rather than having any confidence in their actual abilities.
Some friendships are like a marriage, others like an affair;
the latter are for pleasure, the former for the abundant
success they engender. Few are friends because of you
yourself, many because of your good fortune. A friend's
true understanding is worth more than the many good
wishes of others. Make friends by choice, then, not by
chance. A wise friend can prevent troubles, a foolish one
can cause them. And don't wish friends too much good
fortune, if you don't want to lose them.

*

Know how to use your friends. This requires its own art of
discretion. Some are useful at a distance, others close to
hand, and someone who is perhaps no good for conversation will be as a correspondent. Distance removes
defects that are intolerable close up. You shouldn't simply
seek enjoyment from friendship, but profit, for it should
have the three qualities of goodness, though others argue
it should have those of being – which is one, good and
true – since a friend is all things. Few are capable of being
good friends, and not knowing how to choose them
makes their actual number even fewer. Knowing how to
keep friends is harder than acquiring them. Look for
friends who will last, and although they will be new at

33

first, take satisfaction in knowing they will be old friends in time. The best are undoubtedly those most seasoned – although you may need to share a bushel of salt with them to reach this point. There's no desert like a life without friends: friendship multiplies blessings and divides troubles. It's the only remedy for bad fortune and is an oasis of comfort for the soul.

*

Talk circumspectly. With rivals, through caution; with everyone else, through decorum. There's always time to utter a word, but not to take it back. You should speak as wills are written, for the fewer the words, the fewer the disputes. Use occasions that don't matter to practise for those that do. Mystery has a hint of the divine about it. The loquacious are more easily conquered and convinced.

*

Know how to triumph over envy and malevolence. Showing contempt, even if prudent, achieves little; being polite is much better. Nothing is more worthy of applause than speaking well of someone who speaks ill of you, and no revenge more heroic than merit and talent conquering and tormenting envy. Each blessing is a further torture to ill will, and the glory of those envied is a personal hell to the envious. The greatest punishment is making your good fortune their poison. An envious person doesn't die straight off, but bit by bit every time the person envied receives applause, the enduring fame of one rivalling the punishment of the other, the former in everlasting glory, the latter everlasting torment. Fame's trumpet heralds one person's immortality and announces another's death – a sentence to hang by envy's anxious rope.

*

Never let compassion for the unfortunate earn you the disfavour of the fortunate. One person's misfortune is normally another's good fortune, for there can never be a lucky person without many unlucky ones. The unfortunate tend to attract the goodwill of people who want to compensate them for fortune's lack of favour with their own worthless favour. And it has sometimes been known for a person who was hated by everyone whilst they prospered to gain everyone's compassion in adversity; desire for revenge against the exalted turns to compassion for the fallen. But a shrewd person must pay close attention to fortune's shuffling of the cards. Some always side with the unfortunate, sidling up to them in their misfortune having previously shunned them when they enjoyed good fortune. This perhaps suggests innate nobility, but not an ounce of shrewdness.

*

Take more care not to fail once than to succeed a hundred times. Nobody looks at the sun when it's shining, everyone when

35

it's eclipsed. The masses, ever critical, will not recount your successes, only your failures. The bad are better known through gossip than the good are through acclaim. Many people were never heard of until they went astray, and all our successes will never be enough to negate a single, tiny blemish. Let nobody be under any illusion: malevolence will point out every bad thing you do, but not a single good one.

*

Don't be brittle as glass in dealing with people. And especially with friends. Some people crack easily, revealing their fragility. They fill up with offence and fill others with annoyance. They reveal a nature so petty and sensitive that it tolerates nothing, in jest or in earnest. The slightest thing offends them, so insults are never necessary. Those who have dealings with them have to tread carefully, always attending to their sensibilities and adjusting to their temperaments, since the slightest snub annoys them. They are completely self-centred, slaves to their own pleasure, in pursuit of which they'll trample over everything, and idolaters of punctiliousness. Be instead like a lover, whose condition is akin to the diamond in its endurance and resistance.

*

Don't live in a hurry. To know how to parcel things out is to know how to enjoy them. With many people their happiness is all over with life still to spare. They waste happy moments, which they don't enjoy, and then want to go back later when they find themselves so far down the road. They are life's postilions, adding their own headlong rush to time's inexorable march. They want to devour in a day what could barely be digested in a lifetime. They anticipate every happiness, bolt down the years still to come, and since they're always in such a rush, quickly finish everything. Moderation is necessary even in our desire for knowledge so as not to know things badly. There are more days than joys to fill them. Take enjoyment slowly and tasks quickly. It's good when tasks are completed, but bad when happiness is over.

*

Never be ruled by what you think your enemy should do. Fools never do what a sensible person thinks they will, because they can't discern what's best. Neither will those with discretion, because they will want to hide their intentions which may have been discerned and even anticipated. The *pro* and the *contra* of every matter should be thought through and both sides analysed, anticipating the different courses things may take. Opinions vary: let impartiality be attentive not so much to what will happen as to what may.

*

Without lying, don't reveal every truth. Nothing requires more care than the truth, which is an opening up of the heart. It's as necessary to know how to reveal it as to conceal it. With a single lie, a reputation for integrity is lost: deceit is viewed as a fault, and a deceiver as false, which is worse. Not all truths can be spoken: some because they are important to me, others to someone else.

*

Don't hold opinions doggedly. Every fool is utterly convinced, and everyone utterly convinced is a fool, and the more mistaken their opinion, the greater their tenacity. Even when the evidence is clear, it's sensible to yield, for the correctness of your position will not go unnoticed, and your politeness will be recognized. More is lost with stubborn insistence than can be gained by winning; this is not to defend truth, but vulgarity. There are those who are completely stubborn, difficult to convince, incurably vehement; when caprice and conviction are found together, they are always indissolubly wed to folly. Your will must be tenacious, not your judgement. There are, however, exceptions when you mustn't lose and be doubly defeated, once in the argument, and again in its consequences.

*

Anything popular, do yourself; anything unpopular, use others to do it. With the one you garner affection, with the other you deflect hatred. The great are fortunate in their generosity, since for them, doing good is more pleasurable than receiving it. Rarely do you upset someone without upsetting yourself, either through compassion or remorse. Those at the top necessarily have to reward or punish. Let good things come directly, bad ones indirectly. Have something to deflect hatred and slander, the blows of the disgruntled. Common anger is normally like an angry dog which, not knowing the reason for its pain, attacks the instrument that inflicts it simply because this, though not the ultimate cause, is close at hand.

*

A truly peaceable person is a person with a long life. To live, let live. The peaceable not only live, but reign. You should see and hear, but remain silent. A day without an argument leads to a sleep-filled night. To live a lot and to enjoy life is to live twice: this is the fruit of peace. A person has everything who cares nothing about what matters little. There's no greater absurdity than taking everything seriously. Similarly, it's stupid to take things to heart that don't concern you, and not to take to heart those that are important.

*

Know your lucky star. There's nobody so hopeless that they don't have one, and if you are unfortunate, it's because you don't know which it is. Some are close to princes and the powerful without knowing how or why, except that their luck brought them this favour; all that remains is for their own hard work to help it along. Others find themselves smiled on by the wise. One person is more acceptable in one country than another, and better regarded in this city than that. People will have better luck in one job or position than in others for which they have equal or even identical qualities. Luck shuffles the cards as and when it wants. Let everyone know their lucky star as well as their abilities, for this is a matter of winning or losing. Know how to follow it and help it; never swap it or you will wander off course.

*

Know how to transplant yourself. There are people only valued when they move to other countries, especially in top positions. Countries are stepmothers to their eminent children; envy reigns there as over its own land, and the imperfections with which someone started are remembered more than the greatness they ended up achieving. A pin became valuable travelling from the old world to the new, and a piece of glass led to diamonds being scorned when it was transported. Anything foreign is valued, either because it comes from a distance or because it's only encountered perfect and complete. We have all seen individuals who were utterly scorned in their own backyards and who are now the toast of the world, held in high esteem by their countrymen because their deeds are followed from a distance, and by foreigners because they come from afar. A statue on an altar will never be venerated by someone who knew it as a tree trunk in a garden.

*

Undertake what's easy as if it were hard, and what's hard as if it were easy. In the first case, so that confidence doesn't make you careless; in the second, so that lack of confidence doesn't make you discouraged. It takes nothing more for something not to be done than thinking that it is. Conversely, diligence removes impossibilities. Don't think over great undertakings, just seize them when they arise, so that consideration of their difficulty doesn't hold you back.

*

In heaven, everything is good; in hell, everything bad. In the world, since it lies between the two, you find both. We are placed between two extremes, and so participate in both. Good and bad luck alternate; not all is happy, nor all hostile. This world is a zero: on its own, it's worth nothing; joined to heaven, a great deal. Indifference to its variety constitutes good sense – the wise are never surprised. Our life is arranged like a play, everything will be sorted out in the end. Take care, then, to end it well.

*

Know how to contradict. This is provocation's great strategy, getting others to open up without opening up yourself. It's a unique form of coercion which makes hidden feelings fly out. Lukewarm belief is an emetic for secrets, a key to the most securely locked heart. It subtly probes both will and judgement. Scorn shrewdly expressed towards someone's veiled language is the way to hunt the deepest secrets, drawing these out until they trip off the tongue and are caught in the nets of artful deceit. When someone circumspect shows reserve, this makes someone cautious throw theirs away, revealing what they think in their otherwise inscrutable hearts. A feigned doubt is curiosity's subtlest picklock, enabling it to learn whatever it wants. Even where learning is concerned, contradiction is the pupil's strategy to make the teacher put all their effort into explaining and justifying the truth: a mild challenge leads to consummate instruction.

*

Neither love nor hate forever. Trust in today's friends as if tomorrow's worst enemies. Since this actually happens, anticipate it happening. You should never give arms to friendship's turncoats, since they'll wage a devastating war with them. With enemies, in contrast, always leave the door open for reconciliation, gallantry's door being the most effective. Sometimes an earlier act of revenge has subsequently caused torment, and pleasure in the harm done to our enemy, sorrow.

*

Don't be known for artifice, although you can't live without it now. Be prudent rather than astute. Everyone likes plain dealing, but not everyone practises it themselves. Don't let sincerity end up as extreme simplicity, nor shrewdness as astuteness. Be revered as wise rather than feared as calculating. Sincere people are loved, but deceived. The greatest artifice may be to conceal such artifice, for it's always viewed as deceit. Openness flourished in the age of gold; malice does in this age of iron. The reputation of someone who knows what they should do is an honourable one and inspires trust; that of someone full of artifice is false and provokes suspicion.

*

Know how to divide up your life wisely, not as things arise, but with foresight and discrimination. Life is arduous without any breaks, like a long journey without any inns. Learned variety makes it pleasant. Spend the first part of a fine life in communication with the dead. We are born to know and to know ourselves, and books reliably turn us into people. Spend the second part with the living: see and examine all that's good in the world. Not everything can be found in one country; the universal Father has shared out his gifts and sometimes endows the ugliest with the most. Let the third stage be spent entirely with yourself: the ultimate happiness, to philosophize.

*

Don't entrust your reputation to another without having their honour as security. Keeping silent should be to each other's

43

advantage; speaking out to each other's detriment. Where honour is concerned, dealings must cut both ways, so that each looks after the other's reputation. You should never trust anyone; and if on occasion you have to, do so with such skill that you encourage caution even more than prudence. The risk should be equal and the matter mutual, so that someone who says they're your partner doesn't turn witness against you.

*

Know how to ask. There's nothing more difficult for some, or more easy for others. There are some who don't know how to refuse; with such people, no picklock is necessary. There are others whose first word on every occasion is 'no'; with these people, you need real skill. And with everyone, the right moment: catch them when they're in good spirits, when their bodies or their minds are satisfied. Unless the listener's careful attention detects the petitioner's subtlety, then happy days are the days when favours are granted, for inner happiness streams outwards. Don't go near when you see someone else has been refused, for any fear of saying 'no' will have vanished. There's no good time when people are down. Placing someone under an obligation beforehand is a good bill of exchange, unless you're dealing with someone base.

*

Grant something as a favour before it has to be given as a reward.
This is a skill of great politicians. Granting favours before
they are merited is proof of an honourable person. A
favour in advance is doubly excellent: the speed of the
giver places the recipient under a greater obligation. A
gift given afterwards is due payment; the same beforehand
becomes an obligation. This is a subtle way of transform-
ing obligations, for what was for the superior an obligation
to reward becomes for the recipient an obligation to repay.
This is the case with honourable people. With base individuals, a reward paid early is more of a bit than a spur.

*

Know how to appear the fool. The wisest sometimes play
this card, and there are times when the greatest knowledge consists in appearing to lack knowledge. You
mustn't be ignorant, just feign ignorance. With fools,
being wise counts for little, and similarly with madmen,
being sane: you need to talk to everyone in their own
language. The person who feigns stupidity isn't a fool,
just the person who suffers from it. Whilst real stupidity
is just simple, feigned stupidity isn't, for genuine artifice
is involved here. The only way to be well loved is to put
on the skin of the most stupid of animals.

*

Take a joke, but don't make someone the butt of one. The first
is a form of politeness; the second, of audacity. Whoever

45

gets annoyed at some fun appears even more like a beast than they actually are. An excellent joke is enjoyable; to know how to take one is a mark of real character. Getting annoyed simply prompts others to poke fun again and again. Know how far to take a joke, and the safest thing is not to start one. The greatest truths have always arisen from jokes. Nothing demands greater care and skill: before making a joke, know just how far someone can take one.

*

Don't be completely dove-like. Let the craftiness of the snake alternate with the simplicity of the dove. There's nothing easier than deceiving a good person. The person who never lies is more ready to believe, and one who never deceives is more trusting. Being deceived is not always the result of stupidity, but sometimes of simple goodness. Two types of people often foresee danger: those who have learnt from experience, very much to their own cost, and the astute, very much to the cost of others. Let shrewdness be as versed in suspicion as astuteness is in intrigue, and don't try to be so good that you create opportunities for someone else to be bad. Be a combination of the dove and the serpent; not a monster, but a prodigy.

*

Don't offer an apology to someone who hasn't asked for one. And even if one is asked for, an over-the-top apology is like an admission of guilt. To apologize before it's necessary is to accuse yourself, and to be bled when healthy is to attract ill health and ill will. An excuse in advance awakens suspicion. Nor should a sensible person reveal their awareness of someone else's suspicions – this is to go looking for offence. They should try instead to refute these with the honesty of their actions.

*

Know how to do good: in small amounts, and often. An obligation should never be greater than someone's ability to fulfil it. Whoever gives a great deal is not giving but selling. Gratitude should not be placed in an impossible position; if it is, relations will be broken off. All it takes to lose many people is to place them under too much of an obligation: being unable to fulfil it, they'll back away, and since they are under it, they'll end up as enemies. The idol never wants to see before it the sculptor who created it, nor does someone under an obligation want to see their benefactor. The subtle art of giving: it should cost little, but be greatly desired, and hence greatly appreciated.

*

Never break off relations, because reputation is always damaged by this. Anyone makes a good enemy, not so a friend; few can do good, but almost everyone harm. The day the eagle broke with the beetle, its nest wasn't safe even in Jupiter's bosom. Hidden enemies, who wait for

47

such opportunities, use a declared enemy to stoke the fires for them. Former friends make the worst enemies: they lay the blame for their misplaced esteem on your failings. Those looking on speak as they think and think as they wish, condemning both sides either for lacking foresight at the start of the friendship or for precipitousness at its end, and for lacking good sense in both instances. If a break is necessary, let it be forgivable, done with a cooling of favour, not a violent rage. The saying concerning a graceful retreat is relevant here.

*

You will never belong entirely to someone else nor they to you. Neither ties of blood, nor friendship, nor the most pressing obligation are sufficient for this, for there's a big difference between opening your heart and surrendering your will. Even the greatest intimacy has its limits, and the laws of courtesy are not offended by this. A friend always keeps some secret to himself and a son conceals something from his father. You conceal things from some people that you reveal to others, and vice versa, and by thus distinguishing between people, you end up revealing everything and withholding everything.

*

Know how to forget. This is more a matter of luck than skill. The things which should most be forgotten are the ones most remembered. Not only is memory base in failing when it's most needed, but stupid in turning up when it's best not to: it's meticulous with things that cause sorrow, and carefree with those that cause pleasure. Sometimes the remedy for misfortune consists in forgetting it – but we forget the remedy. It's therefore best to train our memory in good habits, because it can give us happiness or hell. The contented are an exception here, for in their state of innocence they enjoy their simple happiness.

*

Silken words, and a mild nature. Arrows pierce the body, but harsh words the soul. A pill can make your breath smell sweet, and to know how to sell air is one of life's subtlest skills. Most things are bought with words, and they're enough to achieve the impossible. All our dealings are in air, and the breath of a prince greatly inspires. So your mouth should always be full of sugar to sweeten your words so that they taste good even to your enemies. The only way to be loved is to be sweet-natured.

*

Know how to renew your character using nature and art. They say that our nature changes every seven years: let this improve and enhance your taste. After the first seven years we gain the use of reason; let there be a new perfection with each successive period. Observe this natural process to help it along, and expect others to improve as well. Thus many change their behaviour with their status or position, and sometimes this is not noticed until the full extent of such a change is apparent. At twenty, a person is a peacock; at thirty, a lion; at forty, a camel; at fifty, a snake; at sixty, a dog; at seventy, a monkey; and at eighty, nothing.

*

Show yourself off. It allows your qualities to shine. Each of these has its moment: seize it, for none can triumph every day. There are splendid individuals in whom the least accomplishment shines greatly and the greatest dazzles, provoking wonder. When display is joined to eminence, it's held to be prodigious. There are showy nations, and the Spanish surpass all in this. Light came first to enable all creation to shine. Display causes great satisfaction, makes good what's missing, and gives everything a second being, especially when grounded in reality. Heaven, which gives perfection, provides for its display, for one without the other would be unnatural. There's an art to all display; even what's truly excellent depends on circumstance and isn't always opportune. When the time isn't right, then display misfires. No quality should be less without affectation, and this always causes its downfall, since display is always close to vanity, and vanity to contempt. It should always be restrained so as not to end up being vulgar, and among the wise, excess has always been somewhat disparaged. It often consists in an eloquent silence, in a nonchalant show of perfection, for deft concealment is the most praiseworthy type of display, an apparent lack inciting profound curiosity. It's a great skill not to reveal perfection in its entirety straight off, but rather gradually to display it. Let one quality be a guarantee of a greater one, and applause for the first, an expectation of those to follow.

*

Don't meddle, and you won't be spurned. Respect yourself, if you want to be respected. Be sparing rather than lavish with your presence. Arrive when wanted, and you'll be well received; never come unless called, nor go unless sent. Someone who gets involved on their own initiative receives all the ill-will if they fail, and none of the thanks if they succeed. A meddler is the target of scorn, and since they brazenly interfere, they are discarded ignominiously.

*

Live as circumstances demand. Ruling, reasoning, everything must be opportune. Act when you can, for time and tide wait for no one. To live, don't follow generalizations, except where virtue is concerned, and don't insist on precise rules for desire, for you'll have to drink tomorrow the water you shunned today. There are some so outlandishly misguided that they expect all circumstances necessary for success to conform to their own whims, not the reverse. But the wise know that the lodestar of prudence is to behave as circumstances demand.

*

To combine esteem and affection is a real blessing. To maintain respect, don't be greatly loved. Love is more brazen than hate. Fondness and veneration don't sit well together. You should be neither greatly feared nor greatly loved. Love leads to familiarity, and when this makes its appearance, esteem departs. Be loved with appreciation rather than affection, for such love is a mark of great people.

*

Let your natural talents overcome the demands of the job, not the other way round. However great the position, a person must show that they are greater still. Real ability keeps on growing and dazzling with each new situation. Someone who lacks spirit will soon be overwhelmed and will be broken eventually by their duties and reputation. The great Augustus took pride in being a greater man than he was a prince. Nobility of spirit is beneficial here, and even sensible self-confidence.

*

Act as though always on view. The insightful man is the one who sees that others see or will see him. He knows that walls have ears, and that what's badly done is always bursting to come out. Even when alone, he acts as though seen by everyone, knowing that everything will eventually be known. He looks on those who will subsequently hear of his actions as witnesses to them already. The person who wanted everyone to see him wasn't daunted that others could see into his house from outside.

*

Leave people hungry: nectar should only ever brush the lips. Desire is the measure of esteem. Even with physical thirst, good taste's trick is to stimulate it, not quench it. What's good, if sparse is twice as good. The second time around, there's a sharp decline. A surfeit of pleasure is dangerous, for it occasions disdain even towards what's undisputedly excellent. The only rule in pleasing is to seize upon an appetite already whetted. If you must annoy it, do so through impatient desire rather than wearisome pleasure. Hard-won happiness is twice as enjoyable.

*

In a word, a saint, which says it once and for all. Virtue links all perfections and is the centre of all happiness. It makes a person prudent, circumspect, shrewd, sensible, wise, brave, restrained, upright, happy, praiseworthy, a true and comprehensive hero. Three S's make someone blessed: being saintly, sound and sage. Virtue is the sun of the little world of man and its hemisphere is a clear conscience. It is so fine, it gains the favour of both God and mankind. Nothing is worthy of love but virtue, nor of hate but vice. Virtue alone is real, everything else a mere jest. Ability and greatness must be measured by virtue, not by good fortune. It alone is self-sufficient. Whilst someone is alive, it makes them worthy of love; when dead, of being remembered.